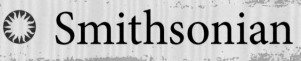

KARL'S NEW BEAK

3-D PRINTING BUILDS
A BIRD A BETTER LIFE

by Lela Nargi

illustrations by
Harriet Popham

CAPSTONE EDITIONS
a capstone imprint

This is Karl
with his new beak.

Garrett

2

In the grassy space he shares with three African antelopes, an Abyssinian ground hornbill named Karl looks for insects and small mammals.

He pinches them between the tips of his long, curved beak.

Then he eats them like any normal hornbill would: He tosses them in the air, catches them in his mouth, and swallows them whole. DELICIOUS!

Shirley

Rogue

Karl shares an enclosure with a type of antelope called lesser kudu. The male is named Garrett. The two females are named Shirley and Rogue.

But eating a meal wasn't always so easy for Karl.

When he first came to the Smithsonian's National Zoo in Washington, D.C., part of his lower beak was worn away. The bone that supported it was too short. This made Karl's beak extra fragile.

When Karl used his beak to dig for food, or when he wiped it on a branch to clean it, the beak would chip. Over time it got shorter and shorter.

Karl's Beak

Karl's beak wearing away over time

So, Karl had to adapt.

Instead of gobbling small, juicy bugs, he could only eat bigger meatballs and tiny mice the Zoo staff fed him. He picked them up by tilting his head sideways and scraping his beak against the ground.

Karl foraging for food with his broken beak

Because of his broken beak, Karl's diet didn't have much variety. His keepers had to weigh him every week to make sure he was getting enough to eat.

They also worried: WAS KARL BORED?

In the savannas of northern Africa, Abyssinian ground hornbills keep busy. They roam up to 7 miles a day on their scaly black feet, hunting.

They might stick their beaks into hollows to rustle up spiders.

They might catch tasty lizards or nibble sweet berries off bushes.

With so much of his lower beak gone, Karl couldn't nibble. And he couldn't hunt the critters that wandered into his enclosure.

Karl was missing out on many common hornbill behaviors. A male hornbill in the wild blinks his velvety eyelashes at the arid landscape. When he notices a venomous puff adder, he POUNCES. He snatches up the snake using his beak like toothless tongs. Then he crushes the snake's head.

He might bring this prize to his mate and chicks in their nest.

Karl couldn't do these things. His keepers wanted to breed him. But Karl's stubby beak made him a poor choice for a partner. How could he use his beak to deliver food to his family? His keepers knew Karl couldn't mate until his beak was fixed. They just had to figure out how to help.

a hornbill practicing hunting using a toy snake

James Steeil, the Zoo's veterinarian, came up with a solution. He molded an artificial beak for Karl out of plastic called acrylic.

He slipped this prosthesis on over Karl's bottom bill. Karl was able to pick up all the crickets and mice and berries he wanted!

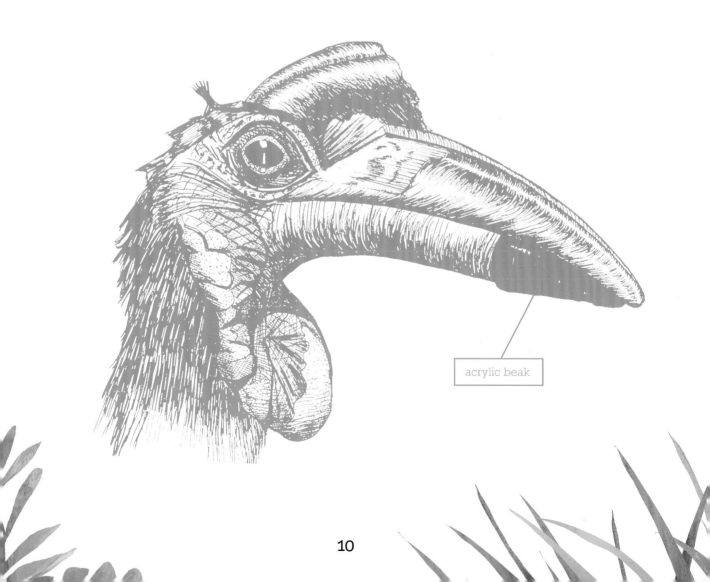

acrylic beak

But the hand-sculpted beak didn't fit very well. And the acrylic
was too heavy. After a few weeks, the prosthesis broke off.

James built another one. Then another. He built Karl ten acrylic
beaks in two years. None of them worked for long.

Then James made a discovery. Across town, the Smithsonian National Museum of Natural History had an old Abyssinian ground hornbill skeleton in its archive.

That hornbill had been about Karl's size when it was alive in the 1930s.

archived skeleton of a hornbill from the 1930s

Could that hornbill's skull help the Zoo staff make a beak for Karl? Could they use it as a template for a 3-D printed prosthesis?

IT WAS WORTH A TRY.

James carefully measured the length, width, and thickness of Karl's beak with a special tool called a caliper. He marked the angle of the beak's curves.

James Steeil (right) and exhibits specialist Bobby McCusker (left) measured Karl's beak with a caliper.

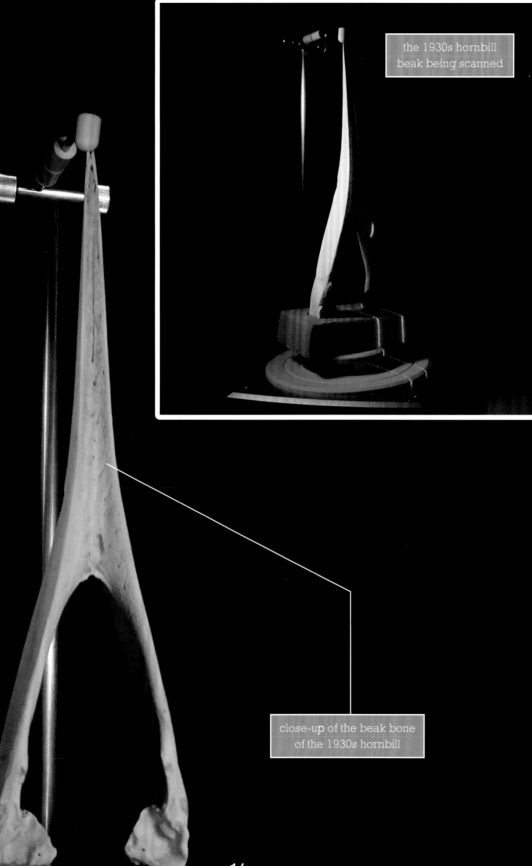

the 1930s hornbill beak being scanned

close-up of the beak bone of the 1930s hornbill

Bobby McCusker, the Zoo's exhibits specialist, made a computer model of the old hornbill skull. To do this, he put the skull into a 3-D scanner. It spun on a turntable. Lasers beamed into its nooks and crannies, taking a picture of it from every which way.

When Bobby uploaded this picture into a computer program, he could change it however he wanted. This would be the template for Karl's new prosthesis.

3-D digital image of the scanned 1930s hornbill beak

Now Bobby had to figure out how to shape the beak. There were a lot of challenges.

For starters, birds' beaks aren't symmetrical. Bobby adjusted the computer model to get it to line up with Karl's unique bumps. He had to make sure the prosthesis would fit over them.

3-D rendering of the hornbill skull from the National Museum of Natural History archives with a 3-D printed prosthesis attached to lower bill

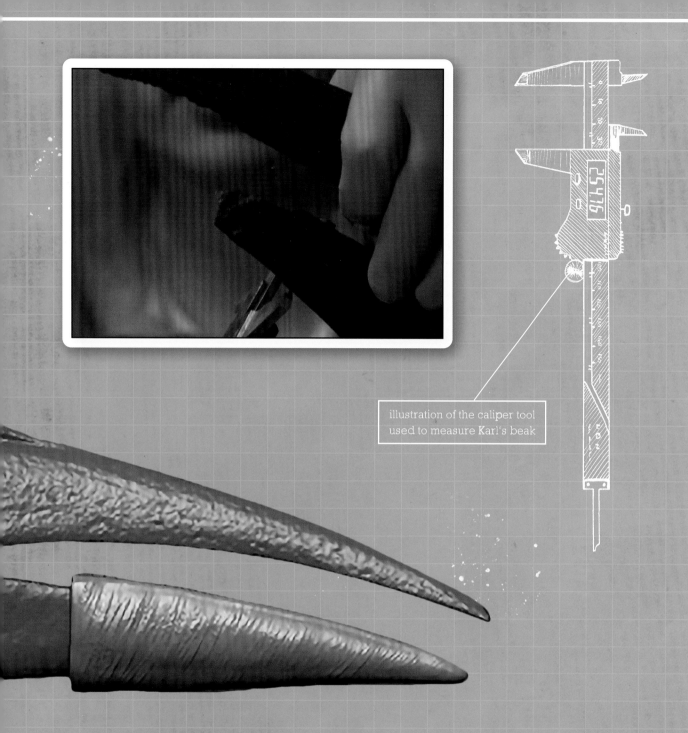

illustration of the caliper tool
used to measure Karl's beak

A hornbill's beak has a groove inside it for scooping up
drinking water. Bobby knew it was important to match the
groove in the prosthesis with the groove in Karl's real beak.

Curator Tony Barthel is in charge of caring for Karl and the other animals at the Zoo's Cheetah Conservation Station exhibit. He knew Karl's new beak had to be both strong and light. He helped choose the material to make it.

Regular 3-D printer plastic bent under pressure.

The toughest printer plastic shattered if it was hit too hard.

The plastic in between was just right: tough and durable, but flexible too.

Now Bobby was ready to print out a prototype. The team used it to experiment with the fit.

prototype in the process of being 3-D printed

The team tested out the third version of the 3-D printed beak.

Assistant curator Gil Myers held Karl while Bobby slid it on his beak. It stuck and puckered in all the wrong places.

Bobby made a second prototype. Then a third. Each time he tweaked and fiddled some more.

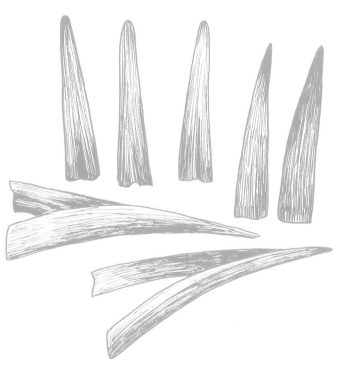

After five months of working out the details, Bobby printed a fourth beak.

They all held their breath as they slid it onto Karl.

test fitting of the final version of the beak

FINALLY, THE FIT WAS JUST RIGHT!

Now they had to attach it.

Assistants held Karl and gave him medicine to calm him so he wouldn't squirm. Karl needed to be perfectly still so his keepers could attach the beak in the right position.

final fitting before the 3-D printed beak is glued to Karl's worn beak

They monitored Karl's heart rate and breathing to make sure he was healthy and safe.

While he was calm, they even gave him a nail and feather trim.

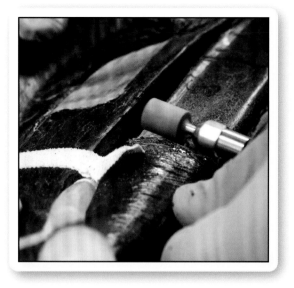

Then James sanded Karl's bill to smooth it. This would help the prosthesis stick.

He marked it with a pencil to show how far up the prosthesis should slide.

James squeezed on glue and attached the prosthesis. Gil held it in place until the glue set. Then James filled in gaps with more glue.

Gil held Karl's beak in place until the glue set.

Thirty minutes later, Karl had a new beak.

The question now was: WOULD IT WORK?

Karl's new beak!

Karl at home with his new beak

Back in his enclosure, Karl rubbed his beak against a branch like he was trying to scrape it off.

But when he saw a meatball to eat, Karl nipped it right up—without tilting his head.

THE BEAK WORKED!

Still, it isn't *quite* perfect. Karl's beak has to be glued back on every few months. But he doesn't seem to mind. Karl spends his days wandering around the antelopes as he hunts for mice and mealworms and crickets.

Karl can eat whatever he wants now, just the way a hornbill should.

He also calls out, looking for other hornbills.

Thanks to his handy new beak, Karl is ready to meet a mate.

ABYSSINIAN GROUND HORNBILLS

(AND KARL!)

Abyssinian ground hornbills (scientific name: *Bucorvus abyssinicus*) are native to several northern African countries. They're a little more than 40 inches (1 meter) tall—the size of wild turkeys. They have wingspans of 6 feet (2 meters) and can weigh as much as 11 pounds (5 kilograms). They're covered in glossy black feathers. Their long black eyelashes are actually feathers too. Females have blue wattles, or throat pouches; males have red-and-blue wattles.

female hornbill

male hornbill

Ground hornbills usually get around by walking or running. But they'll fly into a tree to roost at night, and sometimes to chase prey. No one knows how long they live in the wild. But in human care, they can live up to 40 years. Karl was 27 years old when he got his new beak.

An Abyssinian ground hornbill's most striking feature is its beak. It's about 8 inches (20 centimeters) long and black with a yellow spot at its base. It's topped with a hollow helmet called a casque. The casque makes a hornbill's call louder. A hornbill's beak is also its most important tool. It needs it to forage, kill prey, and eat. A male hornbill also uses his beak to woo a female, banging it on things to impress her and offering her food to show he'll be a good dad. Once he's won her over, he'll bring food to the nest for her and their chicks.

Hornbills mate for life. When Karl came to the National Zoo in 2012 from the San Antonio Zoo in Texas, he had a longtime mate named Klarisse. Sadly, Klarisse died in 2017 from cancer. With luck, though, Karl will have a new mate soon!

GLOSSARY

3-D printer—a machine that creates a physical object from a three-dimensional digital model

3-D scanner—a device that analyzes the shape of something to create a digital version of the object

acrylic—a kind of strong, clear plastic

adapt—to change behavior in order to fit a new situation

archive—a place that stores historical items

arid—very dry, usually referring to a place that doesn't get much rain

breed—to find a mate for an animal to produce young

caliper—an instrument with two movable "teeth" that can measure an object in many directions

curator—a keeper/caretaker of a collection—in this case, a collection of animals

durable—long-lasting

flexible—able to bend or move

prosthesis—an artificial body part to replace one that's missing or damaged; prostheses are more than one prosthesis

prototype—a working model; a try-out before the final version

savanna—a grassy land with a few trees

symmetrical—the same on both sides

template—something used as a pattern

venomous—producing a poison that's injected into a victim

ABOUT THE AUTHOR

Lela Nargi writes books and articles for kids, usually about science. Her first picture book, *The Honeybee Man*, earned a Junior Library Guild Selection, a *Kirkus* starred review, an NSTA "Outstanding Book," a Bank Street "Best Book of the Year," and other awards. Her second picture book, *A Heart Just Like My Mother's*, published in Spring 2018. She's also the author of three middle grade books: *Above & Beyond*, about the history and future of flight; *Absolute Expert: Dinosaurs*; and *Absolute Expert: Volcanoes*. Lela lives with her family in New York.

ABOUT THE ILLUSTRATOR

Harriet Popham is an illustrator, pattern designer, and embroidery artist. She graduated from the Swansea College of Art at the University of Wales with a first class degree in Surface Pattern Design. Harriet makes art in many mediums and launched her own range of products. She has illustrated two coloring books for HarperCollins and created a 40-square meter art installation for a museum in England. Her work celebrates her love of architecture and her family's farming background. She lives in Somerset, England.

Smithsonian Karl's New Beak is published by Capstone Editions, a Capstone imprint
1710 Roe Crest Drive,
North Mankato, Minnesota 56003

www.mycapstone.com

Copyright © 2019 Capstone Editions

The name of the Smithsonian Institution and the sunburst logo are registered trademarks of the Smithsonian Institution. For more information, please visit www.si.edu.

Library of Congress
Cataloging-in-Publication Data:
Names: Nargi, Lela, author.
Title: Karl's new beak : 3-D printing builds a bird a better life / by Lela Nargi.
Description: North Mankato, Minnesota : an imprint of Capstone Editions, [2019] | Series: Encounter: narrative nonfiction picture books with 4D | Audience: Age 6-8.
Identifiers: LCCN 2018029604 (print) | LCCN 2018029014 (ebook) | ISBN 9781684460267 (hardcover) | ISBN 9781684460274 (eBook PDF)
Subjects: LCSH: Veterinary surgery—Technological innovation—Juvenile literature. | Hornbills—Surgery—Juvenile literature. | Bill (Anatomy)—Surgery—Juvenile literature. | Implants, Artificial—Technological innovation—Juvenile literature. | Three-dimensional imaging in medicine—Juvenile literature.
Classification: LCC SF911 .N37 2019 (ebook) | LCC SF911 (print) | DDC 636.089/7—dc23
LC record available at https://lccn.loc.gov/2018029604

Summary: Karl is an Abyssinian ground hornbill with a special challenge. His lower bill had broken off and made eating difficult. Karl did a great job of adapting and finding new ways to eat, but he wasn't getting all the food he needed. His keepers and friends at the Smithsonian Institution wanted to help. Could an old bird skeleton and a 3-D printer give Karl a new beak? Karl's new adventure was about to begin!

Editorial Credits:
Kristen Mohn, editor
Brann Garvey, designer
Kelly Garvin, media researcher
Katy LaVigne, production specialist

Our very special thanks to Tony Barthel, Curator; James Steeil, Veterinarian; and Jennifer Zoon, Communications Specialist at Smithsonian's National Zoo, for their review. Capstone would also like to thank Kealy Gordon, Product Development Manager, and the following at Smithsonian Enterprises: Ellen Nanney, Licensing Manager; Brigid Ferraro, Vice President, Education and Consumer Products; and Carol LeBlanc, Senior Vice President, Education and Consumer Products.

Photo Credits:
Roshan Patel, Smithsonian's National Zoo, Shutterstock: Dane Jorgensen, 28 (left), LagunaticPhoto, 28 (right), SanderMeertinsPhotography, 9

Printed and bound in China.
970

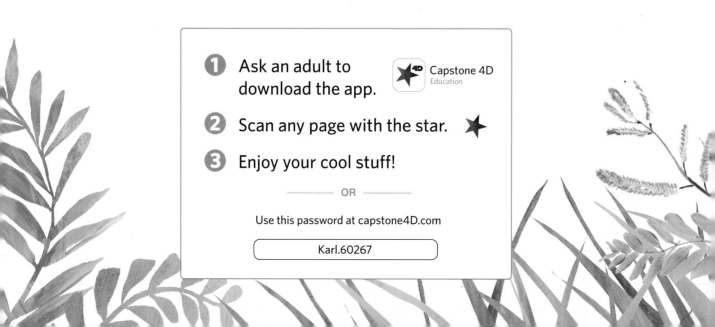

1 Ask an adult to download the app.

Capstone 4D Education

2 Scan any page with the star.

3 Enjoy your cool stuff!

—— OR ——

Use this password at capstone4D.com

Karl.60267